T0104165

Twisters

FIRST EDITION
Project Editor Louise Pritchard; **Art Editor** Jill Plank; **US Editor** Regina Kahney; **Production** Siu Chan;
Picture Researcher Liz Moore; **Jacket Designer** Natalie Godwin; **Illustrator** Peter Dennis;
Publishing Manager Bridget Giles; **Reading Consultant** Linda Gambrell, PhD

THIS EDITION
Editorial Management by Oriel Square
Produced for DK by WonderLab Group LLC
Jennifer Emmett, Erica Green, Kate Hale, *Founders*

Editors Grace Hill Smith, Libby Romero, Michaela Weglinski;
Photography Editors Kelley Miller, Annette Kiesow, Nicole DiMella; **Managing Editor** Rachel Houghton;
Designers Project Design Company; **Researcher** Michelle Harris; **Copy Editor** Lori Merritt;
Indexer Connie Binder; **Proofreader** Larry Shea; **Reading Specialist** Dr. Jennifer Albro;
Curriculum Specialist Elaine Larson

Published in the United States by DK Publishing
1745 Broadway, 20th Floor, New York, NY 10019
Copyright © 2023 Dorling Kindersley Limited
DK, a Division of Penguin Random House LLC
22 23 24 25 26 10 9 8 7 6 5 4 3 2 1
001–333440–Mar/2023

A catalog record for this book
is available from the Library of Congress.
HC ISBN: 978-0-7440-6725-5
PB ISBN: 978-0-7440-6726-2

DK books are available at special discounts when purchased
in bulk for sales promotions, premiums, fundraising, or
educational use. For details, contact: DK Publishing Special Markets,
1745 Broadway, 20th Floor, New York, NY 10019
SpecialSales@dk.com

Printed and bound in China

The publisher would like to thank the following for their kind permission to reproduce their images:
a=above; c=center; b=below; l=left; r=right; t=top; b/g=background

123RF.com: solarseven 1; **Alamy:** Steve Morgan 14, Reuters / Rick Wilking 26-27b, John Sirlin 14;
Dreamstime.com: Andrey Armyagov 29cra, Kelpfish 28-29, Lastdays1 24; **Planet Earth Pictures:** Paolo Fanciulli 9, Alex Benwell 15;
Robert Harding Picture Library: Warren Faidley/Int'l Stock 16-17, 18cl, Beougher 18 br; **Shutterstock:** Minerva Studio 4-5,
Ernest R. Prim 24, Joe Belanger 26-27; **Tony Stone Images:** 20b, Christoph Burki 7tr, Alan R Moller 19; **Topham Picturepoint:** 25

Cover images: *Front: Dreamstime.com:* Solarseven; *Back: Dreamstime.com:* Macrovector Art cla, Tarasdubov cl, cra
All other images © Dorling Kindersley Limited

For the curious
www.dk.com

Twisters

Kate Hayden

Contents

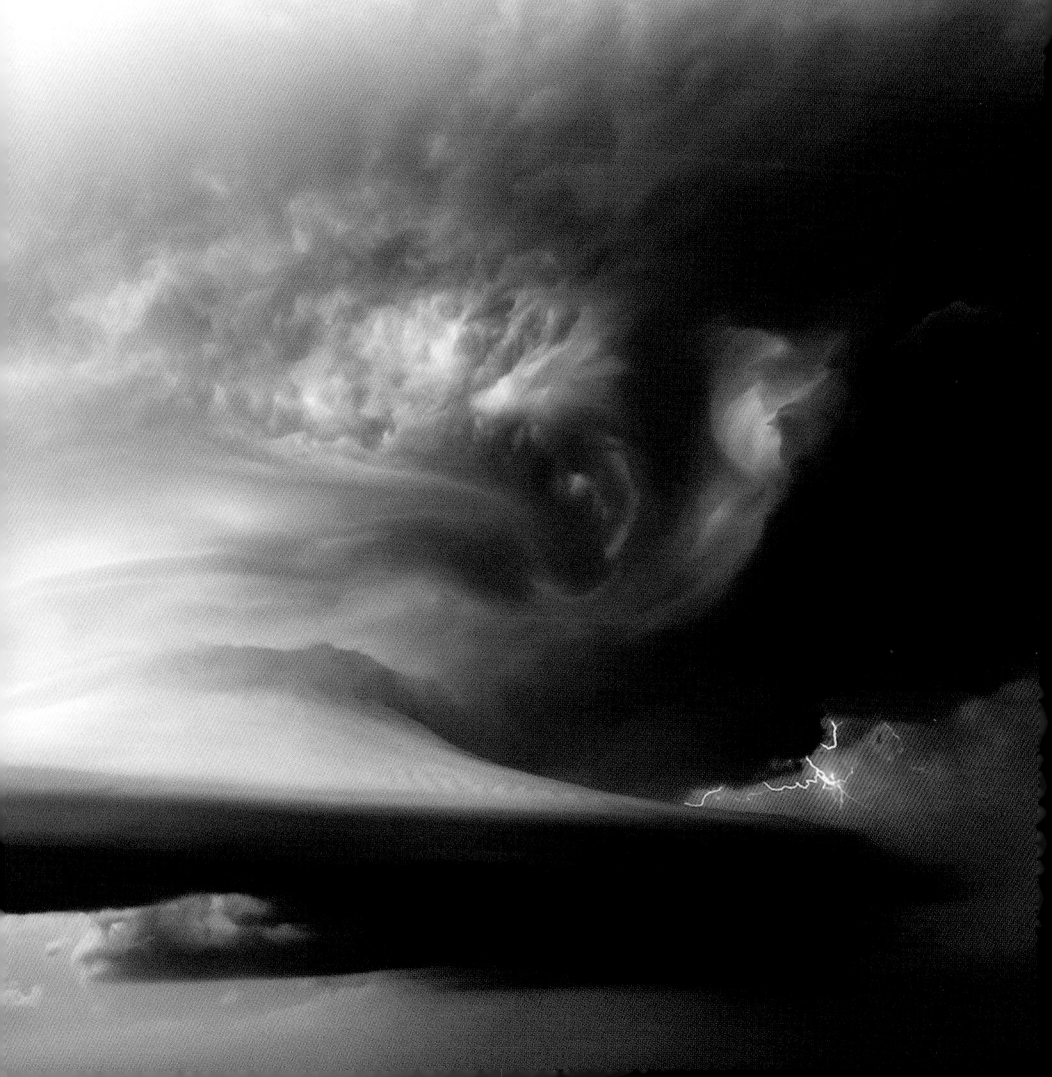

A Twister Tale

Rob was working in his farmyard in Texas, USA. It was a peaceful spring day. But his dog, Barney, was unhappy. He hid under a tractor and would not come out. Rob wondered if Barney was sick.

Second Sense
Animals have sharper
senses than we have. Many
can sense changes in the weather,
like just before a bad storm.

Suddenly, the sky went dark. Hailstones as
big as golf balls pelted down from the sky.
Thunder rolled and lightning flashed.
Then, came a deathly stillness in the air.
Somehow, Barney had known!

A moment later, huge black clouds began to spin. They bubbled at the top, like boiling milk. Gusts of wind blew straw around. Just then, a column of gray spiraled down from the sky. A twister!

Rob stood rooted to the spot. The twister touched the ground. Mud and grass swirled up, like smoke from a bonfire. That was only the start. The twister began to move.
It skipped and bounced across the fields.
It grew bigger, faster, and dirtier as it picked up mud from the ground.

Waterspouts
Twisters over bodies of water are called waterspouts. They whisk up water. The tallest one ever seen was a mile (1.6 km) high.

Suddenly, the twister was hanging right over Rob's farm. There was a noise like a rushing waterfall, then—BANG!
The barn exploded as if a bomb had gone off inside it.

Rob ran with Barney to the cellar in his house. His ears were hurting, and he could hardly breathe. That's because the air pressure around a twister is very low. The low pressure makes people's ears ache and causes buildings to explode.

Just as Rob reached the cellar, his front porch flew off with an earsplitting **CRASH!** Then came a **SMASH** as the house windows blew in. Two minutes later, all was silent.

Rob and his wife, Ann, came up from the cellar. Furniture lay smashed on the floor. Most of the doors and windows were gone. Rob and Ann felt lucky to be alive.

Neighbors helped them clean up. The twister did not damage the neighbors' houses.

Fast and Furious

funnel
cloud

Twisters can form when cold air meets
warm air. The warm air is sucked up in a
swirling column called a funnel cloud.
The cloud spins at a great speed. Twisters
contain the most deadly winds in the world.

No one knows what a twister will do next. It can lift up a large truck and smash it to pieces but leave small objects undamaged.

A twister once picked up a baby boy and set him down safely 300 feet (91 m) away. The baby did not even wake up!

Strange Showers
When twisters drop things they've picked up, strange things can happen. A twister in England caused a shower of frogs.

There are lots of strange stories about twisters. A twister once blew away a man's birth certificate. The twister carried it 50 miles (80 km) and dropped it in a friend's garden.

Another twister sucked up some roses and water from a vase. It dropped them in another room. But it left the vase on the table.

One twister picked up a jar of pickles and carried the jar for miles without damaging it.

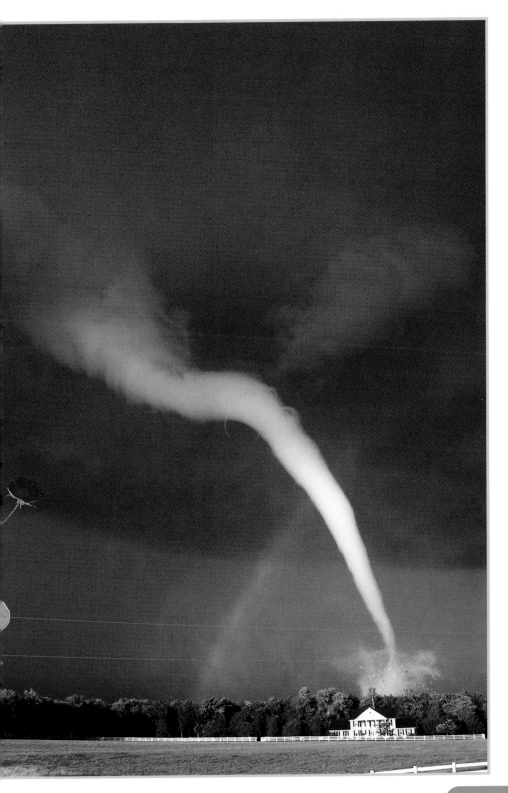

A Close Look

Twisters come in many different shapes and sizes. They can be thin, white, and wispy. Or they can be big, thick, and black.

They can even be in color. If a twister travels across a muddy field, the mud turns it brown—and very smelly!

Twisters can grow bigger and faster as they go along. Some look like they have a loop or knot in the middle.

Some are wider at the bottom than at the top. Some are shaped like a tube. Others look like a slice of pie.

Lots of people have seen
a twister from the outside.
But only a few have looked
inside a twister and survived.

A farmer named Will Keller once
looked up into a twister from his
underground shelter. Just as he closed
the door of his shelter, he saw lots of
mini twisters inside the big twister.
These mini twisters can rip through
a building and slice it to shreds.

Twister Speeds
Some twisters
travel only as fast
as a person walking.
Others travel as fast as
express trains.

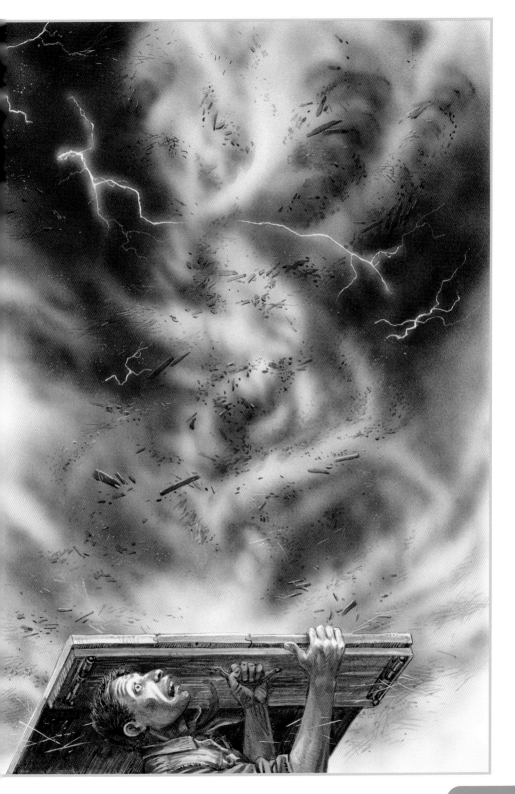

Tornado Country

Twisters are also known as tornadoes. There is an area in the central United States that is called Tornado Alley. It is famous for its deadly twisters. Many violent tornadoes occur in the southern USA as well.

In the USA, tornadoes have occurred in all 50 states. The areas in red, orange, and yellow on this map are more likely to have tornadoes than the areas that are green.

Twisters typically form between April and July as warm air from the south meets cold air from the north—right over these parts of the USA.

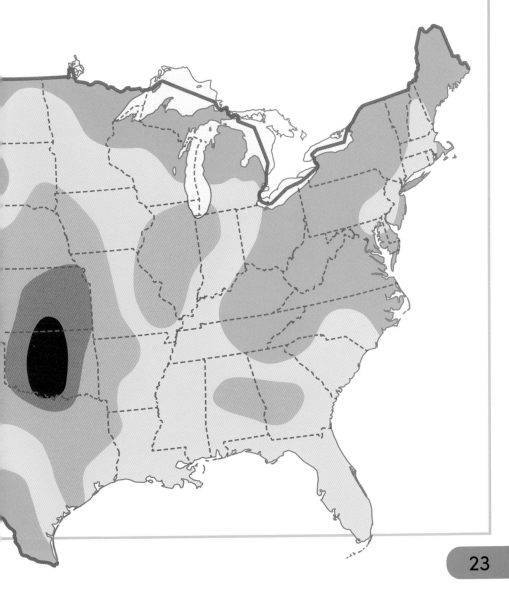

The Enhanced Fujita Scale measures a tornado's strength.

An EF0 damages chimneys.

An EF1 snaps telephone poles.

An EF2 rips off roofs.

An EF3 flips over trains.

An EF4 destroys even strong homes.

An EF5 leaves few things standing.

In 2013, an EF5 ripped through Moore, Oklahoma, USA.

It killed 24 people.

The Worst Twister
In 1925, one twister in Tornado Alley destroyed four towns in less than four hours. It killed 689 people.

People in Tornado Alley are well prepared for twisters. Many of them have an underground shelter outside their home.

The shelter gives people a safe place to wait until the tornado is gone.

People without a shelter hide in a cellar or small room in the middle of their house.

This shelter outside a home in Oklahoma City, Oklahoma, USA, has a stairway that leads to a small room underground.

Emergency Supplies

People keep emergency supplies in their shelters—food, drink, flashlights, and a first-aid kit.

The shelter was not damaged even after an EF5 tornado, the strongest of tornadoes, hit. The shelter kept nine people safe.

Tracking Twisters

Scientists use a computer to help them forecast twisters. The computer makes a picture that shows where a twister is and how fast it is traveling.

Some scientists follow a twister as it moves across the ground. Many of them use equipment such as a satellite dish.

In the past, people did not know when a twister was coming. Today, scientists give people time to find shelter, and hundreds of lives are saved.

Forecasts from Space

Scientists who study the weather are called meteorologists. Some satellites, which are spacecraft that orbit Earth, send information about the weather to these scientists.

Glossary

Cellar
A room or rooms built underground

Enhanced Fujita Scale
A scale that rates a tornado's strength

Forecast
To use information to predict what is likely to happen in the future

Funnel cloud
A swirling column of warm air

Hailstones
Small balls of ice that fall from storm clouds

Meteorologist
A scientist who studies the weather

Satellite
A spacecraft that orbits Earth to gather information

Tornado
Another word for twister

Waterspout
A tornado that occurs over a body of water

Index

Quiz

Answer the questions to see what you have learned. Check your answers in the key below.

1. How do twisters form?

2. What is the swirling column of air in a twister called?

3. True or False: Twisters form in only one shape.

4. What do you call a twister that forms over a body of water?

5. In which parts of the USA do many tornadoes occur?

6. Between what months do twisters typically form in the USA?

7. What is used to measure a tornado's strength?

8. What kind of scientist studies twisters?

1. Cold air meets warm air 2. A funnel cloud 3. False
4. A waterspout 5. Tornado Alley and the southern USA
6. April and July 7. The Enhanced Fujita scale 8. A meteorologist